North American
Animals

AMERICAN
BISON

by Steve Potts

Consulting Editor: Gail Saunders-Smith, PhD

CAPSTONE PRESS
a capstone imprint

Pebble Plus is published by Capstone Press,
1710 Roe Crest Drive, North Mankato, Minnesota 56003.
www.capstonepub.com

Books published by Capstone Press are manufactured with paper
containing at least 10 percent post-consumer waste.

Library of Congress Cataloging-in-Publication Data
Potts, Steve, 1956–
   American bison / by Steve Potts.
      p. cm.—(Pebble plus. North American animals)
   Includes bibliographical references and index.
   Summary: "Simple text and full-color photographs provide a brief introduction to American bison"—Provided by
publisher.
   ISBN 978-1-4296-7702-8 (library binding)
   ISBN 978-1-4296-7920-6 (paperback)
   1. American bison—Juvenile literature. I. Title.
   QL737.U53P683 2012
   599.64'3—dc23   2011025651

Editorial Credits
Erika L. Shores, editor; Heidi Thompson, designer; Svetlana Zhurkin, media researcher;
     Kathy McColley, production specialist

Photo Credits
Dreamstime: Melissa Schalke, cover; iStockphoto: Linda Steward, 7, Stan Rohrer, 1; Shutterstock: Doug James, 11,
Eduard Kyslynskyy, 14–15, Lee Prince, 8–9, Martha Marks, 18–19, Paul McKinnon, 13, PhotoXite, 21, Stephanie
Coffman, 5, Tony Campbell, 17

Note to Parents and Teachers

The North American Animals series supports national science standards related to life science.
This book describes and illustrates American bison. The images support early readers in
understanding the text. The repetition of words and phrases helps early readers learn new
words. This book also introduces early readers to subject-specific vocabulary words, which are
defined in the Glossary section. Early readers may need assistance to read some words and to
use the Table of Contents, Glossary, Read More, Internet Sites, and Index sections of the book.

Printed in the United States of America in North Mankato, Minnesota.
102011   006405CGS12

Table of Contents

Living in North America

Long ago American bison wandered North America's grasslands. Today bison live freely only in wildlife parks. Bison also are raised as livestock.

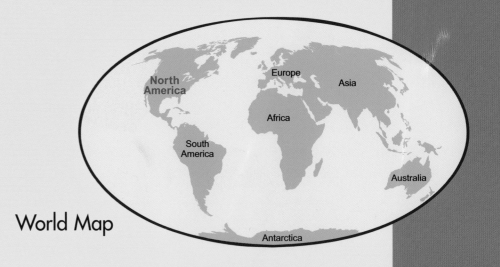

World Map

In 1700, 30 to 60 million bison roamed North America. Settlers from Europe killed bison for their hides. By 1900, only 250 wild bison remained.

North America Map

where American bison live

Up Close!

American bison are one of
the world's largest mammals.
They weigh 1,000
to 1,800 pounds
(450 to 820 kilograms).

Bison have huge heads.

Muscles in a bison's neck

and hump support the head.

On top of its head, two curved

horns point upward.

In winter, bison have long,

thick coats. Bison shed

the long hair in spring.

Rubbing against trees and

rocks pulls out patches of fur.

Eating

Bison graze on prairie grasses and plants. In winter, bison use their heads to push away snow. Then they eat the grass buried underneath.

Growing Up

Bison mate in July. Males fight
each other during mating season.
Only the strongest males mate.
Females give birth almost
10 months later.

Newborn bison calves weigh as much as 40 pounds (18 kilograms). Calves stay with their mothers up to three years. Bison live for 13 to 18 years.

Staying Safe

Today about 30,000 bison
roam wild in national parks
and wildlife refuges.
People cannot hunt bison
on these lands.

Glossary

hide—the skin of an animal

livestock—animals raised for food or profit

mammal—a warm-blooded animal that breathes air; mammals have hair or fur; female mammals feed milk to their young

mate—to join together to produce young

prairie—a large area of flat or rolling grassland with few or no trees

refuge—a place that provides protection

settler—a person who makes a home in a new place

shed—to drop or fall off

Read More

Grant, Debbie. *American Bison.* Voices Reading. Columbus, Ohio: Zaner-Bloser, 2005.

Somervill, Barbara A. *American Bison.* 21st Century Skills Library. Ann Arbor, Mich.: Cherry Lake Pub., 2008.

Stockland, Patricia M. *In the Buffalo Pasture.* Barnyard Buddies. Edina, Minn.: Magic Wagon, 2010.

Internet Sites

FactHound offers a safe, fun way to find Internet sites related to this book. All of the sites on FactHound have been researched by our staff.

Here's all you do:

Visit *www.facthound.com*

Type in this code: 9781429677028

Super-cool stuff!
Check out projects, games and lots more at
www.capstonekids.com

Index

Word Count: 207

Grade: 1

Early-Intervention Level: 19